China-US Relations 2100

By Arthur H Tafero

Forward

Political futures are tricky things. As I mention in my classes, no one can be 100% certain of predicting the future even for one day (See Tafero's Principle of the Certain Failure of Plan A in Google). Even astute companies such as Microsoft have to revise their Plan As over 300 times a year by sending patches to individual computers to revise small apps within personal computers. Most major companies have a hell of a time even trying to formulate a cogent one year budget.

So how can one be so arrogant as to project eighty or ninety years into the future? This book is not about certainties; that would be foolish. It is about mathematical odds, likely scenarios, likely variable changes, and other simple and complex principles. In other words, it is an educated guess, like all books projecting future scenarios. One year budgets for major companies are educated guesses as well, so why should one be surprised for the same process for the path of countries?

There are numerous variables that affect both of these countries going forward in the future. The easiest variable, in my opinion, in the economic one. Both countries have a long tradition of making money, are good at making money, and will most likely continue making money in the following century. The question is HOW will both countries go forward making money.

There are successful businesses that make sensible financial decisions in order to maximize their profits. Net Profit is the primary focus of these successful companies. Unfortunately, countries are not run as well as successful companies (with the possible exception of Switzerland). There are national security and national defense concerns, there are social concerns, there are educational concerns, there are political concerns, there are regional concerns, and numerous other concerns for major countries. That's a lot of concerns and a lot of variables, but they all must be considered before coming up with likely scenarios.

China and the US have numerous strengths, and they both have numerous weaknesses. I have written on China for over two decades and have published over a dozen books on their culture and economics, and I am still learning more about this country every day. I continue to learn about the US every day as well. Both countries have enormous opportunities, and both countries face a number of legitimate threats. So it would appear that a SWOT analysis (Strengths, Weaknesses, Opportunities and Threats) would be in order.

Regardless of all this information, it would still be a monumental task to predict even one year of

1

relations between China and the US, much less the balance of this century. There are just too manyvariables; even intangibles. How do you factor in earthquakes, epidemics, and other catastrophes? Is real life in countries merely a variation of Sim City? To a degree, the answer to that question would be yes.

I am very sure that a good programmer from the Sim City contingent would be able to create a game based on future China-US relations using exactly the same variables that I will be mentioning in this book: Per Capita Income, Unemployment, Trade Balances, Food Prices, Real Estate Prices, Political Changes, Social Problems, social evolution, energy evolution, educational issues, health and welfare issues, National Defense and Security issues, technology, infrastructure, pollution, corruption, financial markets, banking practices and strategic alliances.

These are about 20 basic variables; there are many more, but to keep a focus on likely possible scenarios, we will stick with those 20. There is a vast array of possible outcomes with 20 variables. The final number is approximately 243 MILLION Trillion, or 2,432,902,008,176,640,000. That's a lot of possible outcomes. I have taken a few liberties with a few of the variables in the interest of trying to be a bit briefer and succinct.

Arthur H Tafero

PART ONE - VARIABLES

Table of Contents

PART TWO – POSSIBLE SCENARIOS

Variables

Per Capita Income

Currently, the average American makes five times as much money as the average Chinese. So even though there are roughly four times as many Chinese as Americans, the US has this one substantial advantage in the economic arena. Chinese population is both a blessing and a curse for the Chinese. It allows them to have the cheapest manufacturing costs on the planet, but they also suffer a ranking near 100 as a country where its citizens earn roughly 10000 US a year.

From the latest data, it is estimated, with inflation taken into account, that US per capita will rise slightly in the foreseeable future, but the Chinese per capita will rise at a higher percentage (it almost has to because it is so low right now). Despite the higher rate of appreciation for the Chinese per capita income, it is not projected to pass the US per capita income in this century. Whatever the numbers are in 2100, they should still favor the US over China by a substantial per capita amount.

How does this translate into future scenarios of US-China relations leading to 2100? With more individual money per capita, one receives more individual options. The more options one has as an individual, the more individual freedom one has to make various choices. This is only logical. Individual freedom is generally based on economic power, not political infrastructure. It is wonderful to have democracy, but a rich person in China is much better off than a poor person in the United States.

Americans have more freedom of movement, both internally and internationally, than do Chinese citizens. The infrastructure of the United States is slanted toward the automobile and highways and not mass transportation. In China, it is just the opposite. We will discuss this issue in more detail in the infrastructure section.

In essence, more individual earning power creates more individual freedoms. People who earn $100,000 a year, whether they be in China or the US, have many more options than people who earn only $30,000 or $40,000 a year. US citizens average $50,000 a year and Chinese citizens average $10,000 a year. Therefore, US citizens have several more options than Chinese, when it comes to individual freedoms.

Houses are more accessible to US citizens than to Chinese. Houses are not even part of the equation in China. The country is almost completely apartment-zoned. Living in a house provides more individual freedoms than living in an apartment. You can play the piano at midnight if you like. You don't need to take elevators anywhere. You can park your car in your own garage. Chinese citizens do not enjoy these personal freedoms.

However, there are also problems for the US when it comes to quality of life for those unable to afford a house. The cost of living in China is much lower than the cost of living in the US if you live in the city; unless you opt to buy one of the ridiculously high-priced Chinese apartments in one of their major cities. Over 90% of the Chinese population cannot afford these luxury apartments, and opt for much more reasonable apartment living (about $400-$500 a month) that provide clean and dependable service in family apartment complexes in the vast majority of secondary Chinese cities. Housing in Beijing, Shanghai and Hong Kong are much more expensive, however.

Chinese family units are more tight-knit than US families. This is due to economic necessity. Families of four, five and even six people or more, live in apartments designed for three. Parents and older children often live together with the parents as the primary caretakers of their older children's offspring. In return, the older children provide free food and lodging for their parents. This is far more prevalent in China than it is in the US. US families have become distended and often live in other cities or communities. There are, of course, benefits and drawbacks to both of these living situations.

The bottom line is that US citizens, on the whole, have more economic choices than Chinese citizens, and therefore, have more individual freedoms. Cars add to these individual freedoms, but the Chinese are quickly closing the gap in this area by producing more cars than any other country in the world. Average US citizens generally buy better cars than the average Chinese citizen, because they make five times as much money. American car infrastructure is also superior to Chinese car infrastructure as of the second decade of this century, and will most likely continue to be superior far into the century.

Another quality of life advantage Americans have over Chinese in cars is law enforcement. Americans have much stricter driving rules and regulations for licenses, driving on highways, parking, and other uses of cars and trucks. These laws are strictly enforced in the US, and very loosely enforced (due to a lack of workforce in law enforcement) in China. This makes for a much more pleasant and safer driving experience in the US when compared to driving in China.

Having more disposable income allows Americans to provide better lives for their families as well. Children of average Americans generally get a better college education and have greater access to graduate school. At earlier educational levels, Chinese schools are equal to and sometimes surpass American schools, but at the college level, things go very downhill for China.

First of all, China has practically no community college system. This extremely useful system in the US funnels their top students to four year colleges and allows a lot of students to continue their studies in the summer. China also suffers from a lack of summer college availability in the vast majority of its colleges. The double advantage of being able to go to school in the summer and having an extra bridge to good schools, such as community colleges provide, give American students an enormous advantage over Chinese students at the college level.

Of course, all of these educational opportunities, like going to community college and going to summer courses at most universities, cost a respectable amount of money; money that the average Chinese family cannot afford to spend, despite their heroic sacrifices for their children.

Unemployment and Labor Issues

Right now in 2104, The US is slowly recovering from severe unemployment problems that started around the year 2000. Unemployment numbers are generally cyclical. Countries go up and down with these numbers for unspecified periods of times, having prosperity for a while, then suffering through economic transitions that cost thousands of jobs.

China, on the other hand, has had a nice, very long gradual decline in unemployment over the last thirty years. Their emerging economy has practically guaranteed that anyone who wants to work in China can get a job. This is why thousands of expatriates came to China in the first fifteen years of this century. There is practically always a job in China for a Westerner. People who cannot find satisfying work in the US can now go to China and make a comfortable living. Ironically, Chinese who try to migrate to the US, often have great trouble finding suitable jobs that match their educational and practical experiences in China. They are much more likely to be underemployed than Westerners going to China.

One of the few jobs in demand for Chinese migrating to the US is to become a Chinese instructor at the high school or college level. Other than that narrow opening, the US job market is very difficult for migrating Chinese to penetrate. Another exception would be Chinese students who get educated in the US, who take company internships in their senior years. This gains them entry into the tight US job market. Other than these two exceptions, it is very difficult for Chinese to gain entry into the US job market.

Domestic unemployment is a bit different. China does a better job at putting most of its population to work, while the US suffered from 6-10% unemployment over the last few decades. Both countries suffer about the same rate of underemployment, but there is almost always a job available in China if you need one. Misery loves company, and in China, it is much easier to feel prosperous if you are making 10000US a year like the majority of the population, than it is to make 20000US in the US and be making less than half of what the average American makes. The person in the US feels like a pauper and the person making half that much in China feels prosperous.

The down side of Chinese labor is that there is no social security safety net for the workers. They suffer low salaries (about $1.50 US an hour), low benefits and long hours. These conditions would be impossible to impose on American workers because the American system is far more socialist than the Chinese system. I predict an increasing percentage of labor disputes and incidents in China as a result of this condition with a true socialist movement gaining momentum in the not too distant future. Companies such as Nike and Adidas are being accused of exploiting these workers, but they have numerous suppliers all over Asia. If the Chinese workforce complains or protests too much, these and other companies will merely move their supply orders to other countries where their factories are already operating in similar circumstances, such as Vietnam.

Underemployment is also a serious problem in China. There are several million white-collar college-educated Chinese working in jobs that pay from 1500 to 2500 RMB a month. That comes out to a range of $225-$400 a month. These jobs include work in Chinese banks, schools, medical, social services, and the private sector. Some college-educated grads are even opting to work in Chinese factories rather than accept this very low so-called professional salaries. Salaries in the countryside are even lower than the ones mentioned above. Countryside teachers often teach for food, lodging and less than $200 US a month. These conditions are bound to lead to social unrest in both the countryside and in the cities. Already there is over a 30% increase in protests year on year in 2014 and these work protests will only increase in number and percentage until there is greater parity with world standards for worker's pay. It is ironic that China, perceived by much of the world as a communist or socialist country, is currently in a system that is far more reminiscent of a colony under capitalist control.

The lack of an effective legal system and law enforcement only exacerbates the situation. The CCP is trying its best to cope with these enormous problems, but the scope of the issues is so big and requires so much manpower to regulate and enforce, that the CCP is faced with a Gordian Knot. One possible solution might be to allow freely elected unions and have a second political party in China that is duly represented in the Chinese government (similar to England's Labor Party). This would require the CCP to relinquish some control that it currently has in Beijing. But most observers of China do not think the CCP will give up any of their centralized power without a great deal of turmoil first. That turmoil is already well on its way.

Trade Balance Issues

   Trade balances, like most other variables for countries, are cyclical. In the current cycle, China is enjoying a highly favorable trade balance over the last twenty years or so, while the US has seen a decline in its exports. But like most things cyclical, this will all eventually change over a relatively long period of time; say ten to twenty years down the line. China will begin to see a decline in its trade balance and the US will find new products and markets to return to the positive side of the cycle. And then the countries will reverse their fortunes once or twice more before the century is out.

Here are some facts about trade for the US and China.

Sales and Manufacturing Leaders

1. China is the manufacturing leader in the world as of 2014.
2. China is the leading wind and solar power manufacturer in the world.
3. China is the leading toy maker in the world
4. China is the leading clothes maker in the world
5. China is the leading electronics maker in the world
6. China is the leading car manufacturer in the world
7. The US is the leading aircraft manufacturer in the world.
8. The US is the leading tech manufacturer in the world.
9. The US is the leading energy manufacturer in the world (per capita by about a ratio of four to one over China); China produces slightly more energy than the US (about 2%), but it has four times as many people using the energy.
10. The US is the leading service sector provider in the world.
11. The US is the leading real estate developer in the world.
12. The US is the leading space technology leader in the world.
13. The US is the leading food producer in the world and produces over three times as much food as China with less than one fourth of China's population.
14. The US manufactures approximately five times the weapons that China makes.
15. The US is ranked generally between the seventh to ninth richest country in the world.
16. China is ranked generally between the 92nd to 98th richest country in the worlds. (PCI)
17. China PCI is approximately 9050-9300 US per year.
18. US PCI is approximately 50,000- 51000 US per year. The average American is over five times richer than the average Chinese person. If trends continue for the next twenty years, the average Chinese will eventually be one fourth as rich as the average American.
19. The US is the leading banking sector in the world; the world uses dollars as its primary measurement. The RMB is not yet officially recognized as a world currency.
20. The economic reality: China is still a developing country and PCI must at least double before it

can seriously challenge Western countries, much less the US for economic supremacy. It will take a minimum of forty years for China to challenge, IF Chinese growth continues and US growth remains smaller. However, that trend is already experiencing some changes, and the US economy is recovering in 2014.

What deductions can we conclude from this data? After a few years of unforeseen events, all bets are off, but if the current trends continue we could have:

1. China continuing to be the leading manufacturer in the world because of its population. Unfortunately, the downside of this situation is that the manufacturing will be mostly of low-end goods.
2. The US will be forced to retool itself to manufacture higher-end goods in the coming decades. This will lead to a weakening of some traditional American institutions like unions and collective bargaining.
3. China will become the world's leading supplier of low-end goods; the US will be the world's leading supplier of high-end items.
4. China-US trade would naturally benefit from these two diverse markets. However, since the demands of low-end items are much higher than high-end items (there are billions more of poorer people in the world), China would continue to reap economic benefits from this sector.
5. The US, however, would gain a solid foothold as a high-end supplier and most likely prevent China from making any major penetration into this market.
6. Trade between China and the US would increase over the next twenty years to top one trillion dollars. This would profoundly affect other variables of US-China relations such as military interventions, military posturing, national defense policies and strategic alliances within Asia. As we speak, the Urkranian crisis would have had China automatically support Russia in any confrontation with the West; but in the new World Order, China is now supportive of the West in the UN and was against Russian intervention in Ukraine. This is a radical departure from the past, and places China in more of a neutral position than automatically lining up with traditional allies.
7. Increased Chinese and American interdependency might even affect our relationship with Japan to the extent where we reverse various policies in Asia toward Japan. This has happened previously with Taiwan, when the US reversed its policy toward mainland China with the realization there were many more billions in trade to be made with mainland China than Taiwan.
8. As trade between US and China increases, trade between Japan and US will decrease, as will trade between China and Japan. As trade increases between the US and China, Japan will become increasingly isolated in Asia and may be forced to take some drastic measures (like military buildup).

9. Military solutions between China and the US will cease to be a rational alternative in disagreements within Asia.
10. The Chinese like Americans more than they like the Japanese; Americans like the Chinese more than they like the Japanese. Although this fact has not yet translated into military alliance at this point in time, if current trends continue, you might see a change in American foreign policy in Asia. Japan is unlikely to change its current trends toward isolation. In the final analysis, it will be money and trade that dictates foreign policy in Asia, not traditional alliances.

Food Issues

Food staples in China are cheaper than in the United States. Commodities like tea, rice, and pork are cheaper in China than in the US. Noodles of all types are cheaper in China as well. Milk in China is pasteurized, not homogenized, as in the US and is cheaper as well. However, powdered milk for babies is far more expensive in China than it is in the US.

As a matter of fact, powdered baby milk is a skeleton in the Chinese produce market. Some companies have actually been responsible for poisoning and killing dozens of babies with their product. The Chinese government reacted harshly to these incidents by putting several of the perpetrators to death for their actions. These people would have never received the death penalty in the US for similar activities, but the Chinese public approval of the death sentences was over 99%.

Generally speaking, the quality of food in the US is much higher than the quality of food in China. The safety of food is much higher as well because there are strict controls in place in the United States and a lack of enforcement of controls within China due to insufficient staffing of food inspectors throughout the country. Enforcement of all types of laws is a serious deficiency in Chinese society, as they are very dependent on the good manners and great traditions of the Chinese people.

The quality of Chinese meats is substandard when compared to the US, primarily because of refrigeration. There is far more of it in the US than in China. Chinese have traditions of buying their meat freshly slaughtered and then consuming it the same day. Americans very often do not eat the meat they buy on the same day. It has been processed to last longer than Chinese meat. There are more preservatives in American meat. These preservatives cost money that Chinese meat providers are not willing to spend on processing their meats, therefore, Chinese meat must be sold in a more expeditious manner.

Chinese pork is fairly plentiful in all parts of China at reasonable prices, but chickens are much less available. The ones that are available are not up to the standards of American chickens. They tend to be tough and gamy. Chinese beef is even worse than the Chinese chickens. Beef is scarce in many of the provinces in China and is produced primarily in Mongolia, along with lamb, which is far more plentiful and priced much lower than beef. Again, Chinese beef is gamy and tough, although the lamb is reasonably priced and not too bad.

Chinese have a tradition of flavoring their foods with meat rather than serving them as main dishes, as is done in the US. This leads to far less consumption per capita of meat in China than in the US. Many meats are sold on the street like newspapers in China. There is no refrigeration of these meats and buying and eating them is a dangerous proposition. No such activity could take place in the United States.

Eggs, like Chinese milk, is seldom refrigerated and sold unregulated for the most part. Some of the eggs are of high quality and are bright yellow and healthy. Other eggs have a dull yellow yolk, which indicates that the eggs are not very fresh and are of low quality. The low-quality eggs are cheaper and are sold for a variety of Chinese dishes that are not primary egg meals, but are merely added to fried rice. These eggs would not possibly be allowed to be sold in the US.

Chinese milk is convenient, but not as healthy as US milk, which is refrigerated. Children's powdered milk is far healthier and safer in the US as well. Ice cream is gaining in popularity in China, but it is still only at a small percentage compared to ice cream consumption in the US. Again, refrigeration is the primary concern here.

Chinese alcohol is sometimes prepared in a dangerous and unhealthy fashion (quite like moonshine) and has resulted in several deaths. American alcoholic products are far safer and of a much better quality, generally. Sodas and juices are of decent quality and bottled water is very common throughout China.

Chinese baked goods and desserts are primarily sugar-free and not very appealing to Western tastes. This is not for health purposes (that is the end result in many cases), but because these businesses are looking to save money on ingredients. Recently, Chinese baked goods and desserts have achieved a higher quality, but they still lag far behind the West in rich ingredients.

Chinese restaurants in the US serve much higher quality vegetables and meats in their dishes than the millions of restaurants in mainland China. Noodles and rice are the staples of Chinese restaurants. Very few have potatoes or other starches. Sauces are extremely popular and are often superior to many of the sauces in the West. Again, Chinese flavor their dishes with meat, rather than serve them as a main course. These trends should continue for the foreseeable future.

Real Estate Variable

Real estate in both countries is a two-sided monster. In China, some of the most expensive apartments in the world exist in places like Beijing, Hong Kong and Shanghai. A roomy three or four bedroom apartment in any of these cities will easily run you from 5-10 million RMB or one to two million American dollars. The quality of life in these cities is mixed; the air quality is poor and the value received for this amount of money is highly questionable.

Conversely, renting in China is relatively inexpensive and far cheaper than renting in the US. You can rent a roomy two or three bedroom apartment for around three or four thousand RMB a month or $450 to $600. This is far cheaper than any decent apartment you can rent in large cities within the US. Renting is the best way to go in China. Buying a low-end condo or house is the way to go in the US.

Real estate prices for houses in the US are far lower than apartments that sell in China. You can buy a mansion for one or two million dollars in the US, complete with acres of land and a four-car garage. That plays a lot better for value than a four-room apartment with no personal garage and no land. Most Americans opt for a house in the $150-$200 thousand range if they have a family, and from $75-150 thousand for condos made for older couples without children living with them.

As far as investments are concerned, Chinese real estate is far riskier than US real estate. Paying an exorbitant price for an apartment and then selling it for an even more exorbitant price is very risky. There is great potential for a real estate meltdown similar to the one the US experienced in 2008. All economies and real estate values fluctuate; China is no exception.

The United States, on the other hand, have several million properties that are undervalued and that have been repossessed by banks, who are selling them for rock bottom prices. It is almost impossible to lose money in the current US real estate market if you have a bit of patience and shop wisely. Investments in US properties have a much better statistical chance of selling for a profit later on than do Chinese properties.

One of the disadvantages of the US housing market is renting. Rental prices are far higher in the US than they are in China. This seems paradoxical at first, until you realize that 99% of the Chinese real estate market are apartments and over 33% of the US market are houses. There are fewer apartments in the US to rent, so naturally, the rents are higher than a place with several apartments to rent, like China.

Rental communities are better planned and executed in China than they are in the US as well. Since practically every community in China revolves around apartment complexes, the entire infrastructure of the surrounding areas are tailored to these apartment complexes. In US communities, you will have a mix of houses and apartments with the surrounding infrastructure designed for both; highways for

house owners and mass transportation for apartment dwellers. In China, everything is designed for apartment dwellers and mass transportation is for getting to and from work. That is why infrastructure of mass transportation in China is far superior to that utilized in the United States. The US does not even have bullet train service, while China has hundreds of bullet trains.

Political Variables

Both China and the United States have profound political differences; and not only from an ideological standpoint. The systems are vastly different. The United States has a balance of power system among the judicial (Supreme Court), legislative (House and Senate) and executive (the Presidency). To a certain extent, it is a delegate-oriented system affected by special interests and intense lobbying campaigns. But voting still plays a significant part in the democratic process.

China, on the other hand, does not have a democratic process. There are very few voting procedures that have any significance. The top 100 CCP officials are all appointed, as are the judges in the judicial system, and the premier in the executive system. Therefore, there is still some type of balance of power within these three branches, but they are executed by appointed officials, not elected ones.

Some countries may be under the impression that China is a dictatorship ruled by Premier Xi. This would be far from the truth. After Mao Zedong and China's horrific experiences with the Cultural Revolution that lasted from 1966-1978, the CCP set up a balance of power similar to that of the US, which ensured no premier could ever again become a supreme dictator, like Mao Zedong.

Deng Xiaopeng was the first to cooperate with the new system and was quite successful in pushing China into a new open economy that continued under Jiang Zemin and Hu Jintao. Xi Jinping is continuing that cooperation and China has had prosperity for over the last 35 years. This smooth cooperation and quick action in emergencies has served China well in the last three decades.

Meanwhile, the US has veered wildly from the right to the left and back again every time it elects a new president from a different party. When a Republican takes office, the senate and house begin dismantling all of the legislation and programs instituted by the previous Democratic administration; when a Democrat takes office, the senate and the house begin dismantling all of the legislation and programs instituted by the previous Republican administration. And the dance goes on and on, with less than 20% of all legislation remaining constant through any new administration.

This begets a certain amount of instability that is not present in China. Economic variables are adversely affected by this veering process and stunt growth into the very low single digits. China avoids this veering process as everyone is on the same page economically and they often hit high single digits of growth every year. This process for both countries will continue to stay the same for this entire decade unless some quantum change takes place; which is very unlikely. The current trend favors China in the long run.

The ace in the hole for the US is their ability to initiate innovation in several high-quality production areas; something China lags far behind in except for transportation. China still has the world's lowest cost of production and prices, while the US is perceived as a quality-oriented supply base for high tech items. Both types of economies should prosper for the balance of the century.

American political action is generally proactive and intrusive. We like to stick our noses in everyone's business all over the world. China, on the other hand, tends not to stray too far from its borders and takes very few, if any, military actions outside of their immediate sphere of influence. Consequently, they spend much less on National Defense and are able to reinvest that money into economies that can be sustainable in the future. Chinese like to visit other countries and make business deals. The US likes to visit other countries to make security deals with their powerful Army, Navy, and Air Force. One country deals with others as an equal in order to make equal profits, the other country deals from the idea of fear and mistrust. Sometimes these diverse strategies work well for both countries, and sometimes, they are disastrous; especially for the military alliances.

Social Issue Variables

There is a plethora of social issues in both China and the US. Let us begin with China. The number one social issue in China is reconciling the vast income differences between the countryside and the city citizens of their country. The average per capita income of a Chinese is $10000 US, but this is a deceptive number. In reality, the average city resident in China makes about $16000 a year and the average countryside resident makes about $4000 a year; hence, you get the $10,000 average. But do you really want city dwellers to make four times as much money as people in the countryside?

This has led to some very untidy situations for the Chinese government. By the millions, countryside people flock to the cities like Guangzhou and others to obtain jobs that pay three to four times what they normally earn in the countryside. This has some very unsavory side-effects on society.

Sometimes they bring their families and children. These unfortunate people always live in the poorest sections of any Chinese city and suffer from a variety of problems that traditionally affect the poor and the wretched. Franz Fanon wrote of these people in his classic, The *Wretched of the Earth,* a great read. They suffer from inadequate health care, nutrition, drugs, education for their children, housing for their families and job opportunities. Everything mentioned by sociologists such as Maslow as the basics of human existence are lacking within these migrant worker communities.

The CCP has struggled with this problem for 35 years and has yet to solve it. It is a very difficult problem to solve, with several variables and billions of dollars in costs that will be necessary to implement even the most primary reforms. The problem would appear to be continuing throughout the entire 21st century, unless some quantum solution is found; and that is very unlikely at this point in time.

The make-up of the Chinese class system is presently much sharper from rich to poor than it is in the US. There are far more poor people in China than in the US, percentage-wise as well as physical numbers. The middle-class in the US is far higher percentage-wise than it is in China. It is a goal of the CCP to continue increasing the percentage of Chinese entering the middle class and reducing the percentage of those living under the poverty level. The number of rich in both countries is about the same and relatively constant.

Migration from China continues to be a problem for the Chinese government. Although more Chinese are returning to China than they did in the past, several million Chinese continue to migrate to Western countries for education and business opportunities. The US has very few people who migrate to other countries for education or business opportunities. This is another unseen strength of the US economy.

The US, however, is still suffering from a shrinking base of middle-class citizens. The gap between the rich and poor in the US is continuing to grow in all fifty states. This is not a good sign for a balanced economy or stabilization of the middle class. Unless these trends, on a state by state basis, can be reversed, the US will be heading for a two-class system instead of a three-class system, and that would be disastrous for the economy as well as the quality of life for US citizens. To remedy this situation, all legislation should have the middle class as its primary focus; as of now, that is not the case.

Energy Issues

China is pushing their agenda for clean energy out of necessity. Their cities are filthy with pollution. Beijing is one of the most polluted cities on the planet, and the air is 100 times more toxic than air in most American cities. Shanghai and Hong Kong are not far behind Beijing. And another 500 Chinese cities also suffer from major pollution problems. This problem, of course, is closely related to energy use.

China is trying to initiate solar energy via cheap solar panels which are meeting with great resistance from the West, including the United States, because it infringes on the local Western business profits of inefficient and high-priced energy industries in the West. The same is true for wind power initiatives that China has implemented in the last several years.

China has a serious infrastructure problem with highways and cars. Cars pollute the air. So China has opted for putting their infrastructure money into mass transportation that is clean; bullet trains. This has been a wildly successful endeavor for China and is the envy of practically every other country on the face of the earth. China is head and shoulders over the West in this area of energy conservation.

The Three Gorges project helped to unify electricity efforts within the country. The US is also very efficient in the use of electricity, so both countries can be lauded for their efforts in this area of energy conservation. Mining in China is disastrous, so it is very wise for them to import their mining needs from other emerging economies such as Australia and Africa. This will further reduce environmental impact on Chinese air quality.

On the negative, side, however, the ever-increasing sales and use of Chinese cars using fossil fuels will further exacerbate the air quality problems of the major cities of China. Movement away from fossil fuels is essential to reverse this type of environmental damage, but it is yet unclear which way the CCP wishes to go on this issue, as powerful companies such as Sinopec and others have quite a bit of influence within the CCP. The conversion to electric and other forms of energy for cars, trucks and buses is an expensive proposition, but China might be force to bite the bullet here, if it wants to make any significant change to their endangered environments. It is tough to spend money in a city where you can't breathe or have a life expectancy 20 years shorter than healthy environments.

The United States has a similar problem to China with fossil fuel consumption. It too, cannot make up its mind at the legislative level because of the great influence of the US oil companies within the government. The US and its citizens are addicted to cars, highways, and independence of families. This addiction is highly unlikely to change in the immediate future. Whether or not US cars can make the transition from fossil fuels to clean energy is still unclear, but at this point in time, it appears as if the status quo is the safest political bet, and therefore, things are highly unlikely to change at the state or federal levels in the US for the next several decades.

Education Variables

China has a 2500 year tradition of excellence in education. The United States has a tradition of a few hundred years in education, but has embraced technology much earlier than China, so it has closed the gap between the two countries when it comes to quality of education.

Chinese children begin school at two or three years old; the average US child begins school at four or five years old. Primary education in China is among the best in the world, if not the best. Unfortunately, China is not able to sustain this advantage at higher educational levels, such as high schools, community colleges, universities and graduate schools.

Chinese children go to school many more days and many more hours than American children do. They go to school on Saturdays and sometimes seven days a week. And that is not all. Many of them go to school many more hours a day than American students, who traditionally go from 8-4 (many of them only 8-3). Many Chinese students "voluntarily" go to after-school tutoring or programs from 7-9Pm four or five nights a week. The total number of hours that Chinese children dedicate to school ranges from a minimum of 45-50 hours a week up to a ridiculous 65 hours a week. This is done all in the name of Gaokao. American children average about 30-40 hours a week.

By the time a high school senior in China is ready for college, some superior students would have logged in 6000 more hours of education than American students. This goes very far in explaining why Chinese-American students do so well in American schools.

Gaokao is the ancient Confucian Chinese testing system that is used to place Chinese high school students in Chinese universities. There are only a limited number of slots for each university and thousands of applicants for each slot. These slots are filled through Gaokao. Families often spend thousands of US dollars preparing their child for this test that is ten times more stringent than the SAT. The difference between attending Qinghua University and a local university is the same as attending Harvard or the City College of New York.

City College is a fine institution, and I have personally attended Queens College, a subsidiary of the New York State University system. But let's face it; my advanced degree from Columbia University is far more valuable for getting interviews and landing key jobs. The same holds true for Chinese universities. Universities in China that grant MBAs and PHDs have key advantages over universities within the same city that do not offer these types of benefits. I taught for both Jimei University in Xiamen, which did not offer the PHD, and for YUFE (Yunnan University of Finance and Economics), which did offer the PHD in several areas. YUFE has, by far, a much more prestigious academic reputation, and is far more difficult to gain entry into. Xiamen University in Xiamen was comparable to YUFE in Kunming, and offered several PHD options. Only the lower Gaokao scores opted for Jimei University.

Despite these disadvantages, Jimei University became well-known for two outstanding majors; Navigation, which was seldom offered at other Chinese universities (Xiamen is on the ocean), and advertising, which was introduced to the university by an enterprising Western professor in 2008. Eventually, Jimei University has won almost 75% of all the national college advertising competition within China; destroying all other competition including the blueblood universities of Qinghua, Beijing, Hong Kong, Xiamen and others. So advertising within these two genres is still advantageous for Jimei University.

The primary reasons that Chinese parents send their children abroad to go to undergraduate or graduate schools is because they cannot get into the university of their choice within China, or they do not want to participate in the outrageous pressure of the Chinese Gaokao. Also, Western universities offer a much greater variety and freedom of movement that Chinese universities do not offer.

The Chinese educational system also suffers from confusion about community colleges. These colleges go under various names and offer various two-year certificates that can be transferred to four-year colleges similar to American community colleges, but most Chinese parents are not informed about these options. The community college system in the US is far more well-known and coordinated.

To show you the relative difficulty of the Gaokao compared to a simplistic test like the SAT, Chinese students routinely get double 800s on the SAT test, but fail to qualify for premier Chinese universities when they attempt the Gaokao. An American student would have no chance at all at getting a high Gaokao score.

For the rest of this century, the Gaokao should begin to diminish in importance, and Chinese national educational institutions will begin to offer more variety and mobility within and outside of majors than they have in the past. This will slow down the Chinese migration of many of their best minds to the West. This will be a great loss for American educational institutions, but there will still be a core of Chinese who will continue to send their children to America for graduate or undergraduate school. The American system will see less and less a dependence on the SAT test and have more reliable indicators of potential for American college students.

Health Care Issues

This is a very complex issue. The reason is that the average Chinese has a healthier diet and is in better physical condition by age forty than the average American. They have far lower rates of diabetes because their diet does not contain large amounts of processed sugar. They often use honey as a healthy substitute. They use watered down salt in the form of soy sauce, which is far healthier than the use of solid salt of any type. These two elements alone account for much lower blood pressure, lower weight, and better physical condition by age forty.

On the other hand, more children die in childbirth in China than in the United States by a very wide margin. It is far safer to bear a child in the US. On the other end of the spectrum, it is far better to age over 60 in the United States under Medicare and with the assistance of Social Security, than to depend on the almost non-existent health care system of China for those over 60.

Oddly enough, if one could choose their residence internationally with much greater ease, it would be best to be born in the US, come to China for your primary education, and then go back to the United States for your college and graduate school. At that point, you could choose your job options in either country depending on your specialties. That would only be in a Utopian world, however. Then, you would come back to the US for retirement in an affordable house or apartment and premier health care. Again, this is a Utopian concept.

Unfortunately, in reality, you must choose one or the other when living in China and the US. If you live in China, you forego Social Security and superior health care, but you get better primary education. You also have better job prospects in China. In the US, you would suffer from a second-rate primary education, but you would benefit from a superior college system. Unfortunately, your degree would not get you as good a job in the US as it would in China. The good news, however, is that you can retire in relative poverty with excellent health care. These are difficult choices.

Will the status quo be maintained for the balance of the century? Not likely. Either or both countries might make great strides in education, employment, or social services. It is possible that one country or the other might have all of these as advantages; then again, one or the other might regress to having none of these advantages. The most likely scenario statistically, is that both countries will fluctuate in their efficiency in all areas, with neither country gaining dominance over the other for a sustained period of time.

In China, health care varies widely by area. The citizens of Chinese cities get much better and faster health care than those living in the Chinese countryside. To a much lesser degree, the same holds true for the United States, but countryside residents in the US have far faster access to city medical services than do Chinese countryside dwellers.

It would appear as if health care will continue to improve gradually in both countries for the balance of the century. Both countries still enjoy a medical advantage over the vast majority of other countries and China is making great strides in getting medical services to residents of the countryside.

Welfare Issues

China has a glaring weakness in welfare issues. They provide virtually no money for the older population unless that person is receiving a pension that is job-related. The CCP depends on the age-old Confucianist tradition of families providing for older members. This would include food, shelter and clothing, as well as medicines.

The US, on the other hand, has a very strong and traditional Social Security program in place to assist the aging. China is currently trying to implement such a program for its citizens, but it has four times the population of the US, so it would be four times as expensive for them to do so. For the balance of the century, it is far more likely that China will only have a shell of welfare program that, at best, might provide one quarter or more of the assistance that the US provides.

As far as unemployment is concerned, the US has more of it than China, but also provides more services for finding new jobs. China does not really have many job-finding services because there is almost always a job available for someone if they really want it in China. However, there are still millions of Chinese who are grossly underemployed, as well as there are several million Americans who are underemployed. The problem of underemployment may be a more serious problem than employment for both countries.

Training for new jobs is essential to move people from the unskilled labor force to jobs that require a certain amount of expertise. The US does very well in this area, but China has lagged behind in training their work force for anything but factory labor. If you want your economy to be quality-oriented instead of price-oriented, it is essential that you train your labor force accordingly.

Emergency services to both citizens of the US and China are about the same. You get excellent emergency service in the US at public hospitals and the response to emergency numbers like 110, are very good in most areas. Of course, cities experience a better response time in both countries due to the availability of personnel.

In China, a call to 110 is just as efficient, if not more so, than a call to 911 in the US. Again, there will be a quicker response time in the cities than in the countryside in both countries. For bigger emergencies, China comes out a bit ahead on the scoreboard because Beijing and the CCP act very quickly in most catastrophes, while in the US, the states and federal government sometimes bicker over whose responsibility it is for any one particular event. The flooding in New Orleans was a prime example of that possibility. For the balance of the century, there will probably be a status quo maintained by both countries.

As for social services for children, China does very well in taking care of unwanted children. The US often runs into custody battles and other legal problems with the care of children. China keeps custody battles to a minimum and tries to make the process as smooth as possible for the child.

National Defense Issues

The United States spends more on National Defense than all the other countries in the world combined. This fact greatly impacts the American budget. A full quarter of every American tax dollar goes to National Defense. That is a lot of money that is not being reinvested for potential growth industries. China suffers from the same steep cost, but to a much lesser degree. China generally stays within its borders, but uses the PLA for various national emergencies. In the US, the National Guard performs these functionts. The effect on the American budget is much more profound than on the Chinese budget.

The cost of maintaining nuclear weapons is enormous and wasteful for something that is never used. Space exploration is exciting and scientifically productive, but does not contribute immediately to the national economy. Military adventures in places like Korea, Vietnam, Iran, Iraq, Afghanistan, Bosnia, Africa, NATO and other areas, continually siphon tax money that could have been used for research for new energy sources, cures for various diseases, and improvements in both education and infrastructure. The United States has chosen to generally rely on military options, rather than economic sanctions or other options.

This policy has an excellent chance of changing in the coming decades. As economic considerations take precedence over political considerations in both countries, you will see a more pragmatic approach to border disputes, disagreements among countries about their spheres of influence, and international water rights. Military options are a very poor second choice to solving most issues through negotiations and money-saving devices. No one wants to spend money on costly wars.

China has a much more difficult job in guarding its borders than does the US. With neutral oceans on the East and West, the US relies on the Coast Guard to keep an eye on troublesome events. Keeping an eye on the thousands of miles of Chinese borders with Russia, India, and other states is far more taxing for China than it is for the US. The US has its troubles with Mexico, but Canada is not really that much of a problem. So, the US has it easy compared to China.

The US Navy is also far superior to the Chinese Navy. This makes guarding the waters in their sphere of influence much easier as well. The one weakness of the US Navy is that it spreads itself far too thinly across the world in order to be the policemen of the world. China does not attempt to do this in Asia. In the foreseeable future, both countries will probably maintain the status quo of what they are currently doing.

In the area of nuclear weapons, which have become alarmingly obsolete, the US spends far more money on submarines and nuclear capability than does China. Within the current century, we should see a gradual disarming of most of these nuclear weapons, but the US will spend much more money doing that than will China. In the seventy years of nuclear capability, only two bombs have actually been used against another country; none in the last sixty-nine years. The balance of the century should see almost zero chance of nuclear proliferation and usage.

International Relations Variable

National defense issues impact the outcome of international relations as a variable in many instances. If a country, such as the United States, has an aggressive national defense policy, as is currently in force by the Pentagon and the State Department, then international relations become that much more difficult to initiate.

Countries generally find it much easier to negotiate business and other deals with countries like China, that do not impose military pre-conditions before negotiating a complex business deal, rather than countries like the United States, that has certain pre-conditions before sitting down for business discussions.

The media is rife with daily forays by China into dozens of countries all over the globe to make mutually beneficial business deals without pre-conditions. On the other hand, the media is also rife with reports of the latest US casualties in places like Iraq, Afghanistan and other places. The State Department and the Pentagon are very good at placing preconditions before negotiating any business deals for the United States. This severely hampers US business efforts in several parts of the world.

In the 1950s and 1960s, it used to hamper trade between the United States and "communist" countries. In the 1970s, it used to hamper trade between the United States and China. The United States had an unfortunate habit of supporting unpopular governments such as the Diem regime in Vietnam; a Catholic administration of a country that was over 80% Buddhist, the Shah of Iran previous to the Islamic Revolution, and other despots in various countries, because they towed the line for the US State Department and the Pentagon.

The US has gradually improved its international skills since the 1980s. China has improved its international skills as well since the same time period. China no longer robotically supports traditional allies like North Korea and Cuba as it used to in the 1970s and previous. Why? Because there is a lot more money to be made in trade with the United States than ever could be mustered by North Korea and Cuba combined.

China does not openly support countries at odds with the United States like it used to; they just quietly cut deals on the side, such as oil deals with Venezuela, an outspoken critic of the US. The US does the same thing when it cuts deals with Japan, an outspoken critic of China. The financials, however, tell a different story.

The levels of trade in the billions is increasing between the US and China and decreasing by the billions between the US and Japan. This does not bode well for Japan, which is becoming increasingly more isolated in the Asian theater. This will almost certainly lead to a military buildup by Japan to replace the quickly disappearing military support of the United States. This will create a long-term problem for China as well.

China is making several enormous deals with Africa and South America to improve infrastructure and provide jobs for fledgling economies in both continents. They do this for very low prices they pay for the natural resources of various countries within these continents. The United States could have made these deals for their economy, but failed to do so, because of the preconditions required by the State Department and the Pentagon. China does not fall into such silly traps as that.

If the United States can come to their economic senses in the latter part of the 21st century, they should start making the same kind of unconditional deals with countries in Africa and South America to obtain badly needed natural resources in exchange for infrastructure improvements by companies such as Catepillar and others. If not, then China will continue to make massive inroads to market share in both continents and their economy will continue to grow from 7-10% per annum, while the US struggles to reach 3 or 4% per annum growth.

Infrastructure Issues

Infrastructure issues are a mixed bag for both countries. China has the best train transportation in the world and benefits greatly from this enormous asset. Citizens can live hundreds of miles away from their jobs and still get to work in less than an hour. This also reduces housing problems and pollution from local autos. The United States is still in the 19th century for most of its train travel. The train,s are slow and cumbersome and take five to six times as long to arrive at destinations than do the trains in China.

Unfortunately, China's considerable advantage in infrastructure in rail travel does not extend to automobile travel. The United States still has better roads and better maintenance of those roads in practically every sector of the country. The US uses better quality building materials, which, in the end, save a lot of money in the long run. Chinese highways are always in an endless procession of construction and repair due to poor planning and inferior building materials. Rains and snow damage Chinese highways much more often than they damage US highways because of these inferior building materials. The Chinese take pride in saving money and finishing a building project quickly, rather than spending a bit more money and taking a bit more time to finish a higher-quality project.

There are exceptions, of course. The Three Gorges Dam project was meticulously planned and executed with only the finest of building materials and the employment of the finest engineers. The project was not rushed and the finished result was impressive. The US has had similar successes with its Hoover Dam and the Tennessee Valley Authority.

Housing has been a weak point for both countries. The Chinese have built thousands of unoccupied speculative apartment buildings throughout the country. By the thousands, they remain an eerie reminder of unbridled greed by a number of the new entrepreneurial class of Chinese real estate developers, who, tasting earlier success in similar projects, became reckless in their pursuit of quick (and not so quick) profits. These eyesores now dot practically every populated area of China.

The CCP is aware of this problem and is trying to curb its proliferation, but the problem remains and will probably remain for the rest of the century. One solution might be forced occupation of any apartments that are built. This would require people to buy the apartment in advance of its construction. This would be a difficult task, at best, but one that might be necessary for China as it moves forward.

The frenzy of enormous profits in real estate in the 1990s led to the eventual inflation of all real estate in the US by the end of that decade. It also marked the end of highly speculative real estate by large numbers of US citizens; looking to buy and then flip a property in just a few months for a tidy profit. Those days are pretty much gone for good in the US as we approach the first quarter of the century and will probably remain in check for at least another quarter.

Pollution Issue

America is currently appalled at the pollution problems of China in some of their big cities, especially Beijing. America has a very short memory. At the turn of the 20th century, American cities were among the most polluted areas in the history of the world (with London being a close second). The use of coal for over 80% of factories using energy was the primary cause of this pollution in both the US and London.

Eventually, through new technologies and with a bit of luck, the United States was able to clean up its air from about 1920 to about 1950, until the second great wave of pollution, massive car usage, hit the United States in the 1950s. This burgeoning problem is beginning to abate with the growing use of electric, solar and other non-fossil fuel energies, but there is still substantial pollution in places like Los Angeles (where the natural environment is not receptive to massive fossil fuel emissions because of the location of LA between two mountain ranges), New York and other urban areas.

China has a plethora of pollution problems. It has polluted drinking water, rivers, bays and other waterways. It has polluted air in almost every major city. The combination of polluted water and air has led to a cancer increase in the Chinese population that is approaching 500%; that is a very big rise in cancer. A case might be made for under-reporting cancer in the last few decades, but the reported number of cancers in cities and countrysides have risen from about 1 million in 1949 to over 5 million reported cases in 2013. It is suspected that the actual numbers might be three or four times higher than that.

China is trying mightily to release itself from fossil fuels, but still has a major dependency on coal. The never-ending increase of Chinese cars emitting poisonous gases is exacerbated by millions of motorcycles that run on gasoline as well. China has adopted rechargeable motorcycles to combat some of this problem, but many of them are not as dependable as gas-driven bikes. Many an owner of the rechargeable bikes can be seen walking them home or to a building with an electrical outlet for recharging after they abruptly stop working in some very inconvenient situations.

Electric cars and other non-fossil fuel vehicles are now much more expensive than traditional gas-driven cars in China. This practically guarantees that they will be shunned by well over 90% of the population. To be fair, the same is true in the United States, but there is a higher percentage of users of non-fossil fuel vehicles there. Both countries have switched to non-fossil fuels for public transportation and buses, although the process seems to be going slower in China. The Bullet Train does offer some respite for the Chinese masses, however, that the US populace does not currently enjoy.

If current trends continue, the health-care system of China will be rampant with millions of lung and cancer patients during the current century. This will cause the Chinese government to come up with much more severe restrictions on fossil fuels. This will almost certainly impact the economy in a negative fashion and must be considered a major concern of the Chinese government in the immediate future. The United States, it would appear, has the upper hand in this battle against fossil fuels, but it should be wary of other possible disasters, such as fracking and other fossil fuel dangers, as well as oil leaks in oceans and bays.

The typical small American city is very quiet in the morning. During the day there is activity, but, for the most part, by the end of the day, the small city is quiet once more. This is a wonderful scenario for an introduction of a play like *Our Town*, but as far as infrastructure is concerned, this is not a healthy sign. It means pretty much nothing is going on; nothing being torn down, nothing being built, and no progress being made.

The typical small Chinese city is almost never quiet. Activity is constant; sometimes 24 hours a day. There is always construction going on almost on every block of the city. Apartments are being torn down, renovated or built. Stores, Malls and entire shopping complexes are being built within one month most of the time. The pollution is rampant . The noise is unnerving. You would much rather spend a vacation at the small American city, but the Chinese are too busy trying to make money to worry about vacations. And a Chinese city is about the last place in the world you would want to go to take a vacation, anyway.

It is too early in the century to come to a conclusion about the infrastructure of these two giants, but if current trends continue, China will eventually have superior infrastructure for almost everything in the country except for highways, while the typical US citizen will most certainly enjoy his drive to a nice quiet town. There will be plenty of quiet towns to choose from by the end of the century.

Pollution is an issue for both countries. As of 2014, global warming has begun to affect the yearly weather of both countries. Rains are more plentiful in some areas, and much scarcer in others. Snowstorms and ice storms are more severe. There are more tornados, cyclones, tsunamis, and earthquakes than at any other time in recorded history.

The ozone is being depleted at a rapid rate and the polar ice caps are melting at a high rate. The air pollution from fossil fuels make the air poisonous in cities like Beijing. The average life expectancy for members of both sexes is over ten years less than other Chinese cities. The rate of cancers is five times higher in Beijing than other Chinese cities as well. Despite being the political epicenter of Chinese power and the best place in China to find a high-powered job, Beijing currently demands a great sacrifice for humans willing to live there. Few rational people would give up ten years of their lives and an almost certain future date with cancer in order to pursue their careers. But millions do so just the same.

New York City is fortunate to be on the coast of the Atlantic Ocean, and so a great amount of its pollution is blown away into the sea. Still, New York has a high degree of pollution and high cancer rates. Both New York and Beijing are employment and entertainment targets for young people and a place where persons over 50 or so will find the environment more and more unbearable.

Future trends do not look so good. Los Angeles, locked in by two mountain ranges which help to add to the pollution problem of the LA Freeway, should only get worse as a living place for older American adults. The trend away from fossil fuels is a step in the right direction, but the primary pollution of the area still remains. Other American cities experiencing high pollution rates include Newark, Detroit, Chicago, Dallas, Miami, Houston, Philadelphia, Boston, Baltimore, Washington, Atlanta, and Cleveland. China, on the other hand, has over 400 cities with pollution levels above the American cities mentioned in this paragraph.

By the end of the century, there will most likely be one of two scenarios. Either the US and China will come to its senses, utilize green power like wind and solar, rid itself of fossil fuels, cut down on electrical usage and nuclear alternatives, or life in both countries will become substantially more uncomfortable for the older populations. Even the younger populations will begin to suffer noticeable physical degradations. The choice is up to the two countries, their leaders and their people.

Corruption Issues

There is a great deal of corruption in both the United States and China. Interestingly, the corruption is in different areas and poses different threats to the stability of both countries.

At the highest level of government, there is more corruption in the United States, especially those connected with lobbyists in the Congress, who consider corruption no more than "doing business", when in reality, these representatives are selling their constituents down the river for favorable treatment by special interests. Most political representatives will deny any wrongdoing themselves, but few would be willing to publically state that these conditions exist within both Houses at a fairly high percentage.

The corruption in the upper echelons of the CCP in Beijing is of a different variety. Everyone is on the same page, so to speak, in the CCP. There is only one political party and that party is committed (to a degree) to the betterment of the Chinese masses. There is some corruption for jockeying for power positions within the party, but selling out the constituents to special interests is dealt with very harshly within the party. Corruption is far more rampant among minor officials than the leaders in Beijing.

It is at this point in the hierarchy that China overtakes the United States in corruption. Minor US officials at all levels of federal and state governments tend to have less than the international average of corruption among their officials. The FBI, IRS, Social Security and other large governmental offices are generally free of corruption and scandal. The vast majority of corrupt officials at this level generally come from state and local governments, not from the federal level.

Despite the healthy number of corrupt officials in the US at the state and local levels, it pales in number and intensity when compared to lower officials in provinces and cities in China. Corruption is absolutely rampant at these levels in China and has been this way for many hundreds of years. The new PM of China, Xi Jinping, is very big at eliminating corruption, but even with the entire might of the CCP behind him, Xi will only be able to reduce the corruption by a small percentage, as it is so ingrained in the current system that it is virtually impossible to eliminate unless there is massive restructuring of the economy and social structure. This is not likely to take place anytime soon.

The average citizens of the US are no more honest or corrupt than those of China. There is more effective law enforcement in the US, but there are more lawbreakers and crimes as well. At the masses level, there is no advantage to either culture.

Currently, and I use that word advisedly, the US has an enormous advantage over China in technology. Microsoft, Apple, Intel, and dozens of other high-tech companies are located in the US and China suffers from a dearth of tech companies, primarily because they are not currently able to protect the intellectual property rights of the tech developers within their own country.

Law enforcement, due to a massive population and a limited qualified workforce, has always been a national sore spot for China. Their intellectual property right protection is among the weakest of any developed country in the world. To be fair, China is still a developing country, but when it tries to send signals that it is ready to join the tech race with the big boys, there are mostly snickers that you hear in the rest of the room. The one area where China excels in tech, however, is in its use of cell phones.

There is no more reasonable cell phone usage rates in the world than you have in China. The major companies that provide tech within China, such as China Telecom, China Mobile, China Unicom and others, are tightly regulated by the Chinese government. The end result is the lowest cost in the world for cell phone use by the individual. You can actively use a cell phone for less than fifteen US dollars a month in China, and in many cases, even as much as half as that amount. The US companies don't even come close to competing with those kinds of prices.

Computers and software cost less as well in China. You can buy bundles for half the price of US tech bundles, but the downside is that many of the components are pirated, which leads us back to the original problem of why tech companies and talented individuals within those companies do not like working in China. It is a major headache for the Chinese government. How much protection do you give private companies in relation to the wants and needs of the Chinese populace?

Chinese companies are taking their cues from Japan and Korea. They are copying Western technology and making it cheaper and more widely available than their counterparts. This is fine for a domestic policy, but when it comes to exporting these products, China will eventually have a reputation for price rather than quality. Japan already went through this cycle in the 1960s and 1970s. It started with cheaper low-quality electronics, and then developed a quality mentality for companies like Sony and Panasonic. China might be able to copy this model from the Japanese; or it might regress back into the great Chinese tradition of low price before all other considerations.

Another side effect from tech problems is the brain drain on Chinese talent. Young, bright techies in China are painfully aware of the pirating conditions that are rampant throughout the country with no end in sight. They will be going to countries where their intellectual property is better guarded. This means many will flee to Singapore, Japan, Australia, Europe and the US. No country can long afford to lose their best and brightest, so China must come up with a solution to this problem.

Oddly enough, China has a rich history of inventiveness, being responsible for thousands of tech advances in the past (see Joseph Needham's *Chinese Civilization* book series). For one reason or another, they were never able to capitalize on these many advances. The current mentality is to copy something superior, produce it at a cheaper price, and then try to take over the market for that item. In the long run to 2100, this strategy seems doomed to failure and will keep China as a second-rate technological power for at least the next hundred years.

Medical Issues

Both countries have strengths and weaknesses that will have to be dealt with in the upcoming decades. China has a 5000 year tradition of herbal medicine. Some of it is extremely useful and cutting edge, and some of it is purely Taoist fantasy and has little, if any, practical use. The problem with Chinese herbal medicine is identifying and isolating the fantastic medicines that work medical wonders from the superstitious, nonsensical concoctions that actually harm patients in the long run.

Very few medical experts have been able to do this.

As a result, Chinese herbal medicine remains a crap shoot for the vast majority of Chinese citizens who use it. It is a tremendous boon to those it helps, and a cruel outrage of disappointment to those it does not. The promises of Chinese herbal medicine range from providing users with eternal life (an obviously fraudulent mystical Taoist claim), to curing the common cold in less than twenty-four hours (documented by several Western medical experts).

Some of the claims of Chinese herbal medicine are ridiculous and completely unproven. Others border on miraculous and have several documented cases of success. There are documented cures of serious conditions such as various ulcers in the stomach, shingles, heart conditions, brain tumors, and extreme back pain (acupuncture). Unfortunately, there are also false claims of abilities to treat various cancers and debilitating nerve disorders. But, taken as a whole, Chinese herbal medicine offers the world a very good alternative to Western medicine, and for prices that are substantially lower than Western drugs.

Exacerbating the problem for China is an aging population that currently receives precious little assistance in old age. In some cases, retired adults in China receive less than 200 RMB or $30.00US a month from the government. Compared to the average of $800US a month received by American retirees, the Chinese system provides less than 5% of what the American system provides. This gap is even more serious in the countryside of China, where there are far more poor people than in the cities.

The American side of the coin has some interesting problems as well. The US has tremendous health care and state of the art drugs, but most people in the US cannot afford either one. Obamacare has rectified some of this problem, but the problem still remains for the vast majority of Americans. Basically, it is a healthcare system for the middle-class and the rich, while the working-class and the poor are forced to accept inferior health care and inferior drugs.

Both countries could profit enormously from adopting the technologies, health care systems, drugs and herbal medicines of each other, but there is currently a great amount of resistance by both countries to do so. Political and Economic forces have tended to promote the special interests of businesses (American and Chinese drug companies) and powerful organizations (American Medical Association, CCP), rather than the interests of the common man. These same special interests also contribute to the economies and good health care of millions, so it is a very complex problem to solve.

For the upcoming century, the most likely scenario is a combination of these two great systems. The scenario of complete Chinese domination is highly unlikely, as is the scenario of complete Western domination. Political and Economic forces in both countries would preclude the total domination of any outside culture. The trick, of course, is to select the best health care systems, tech, drugs, and techniques from each other; no simple task.

Financial Market Issues

In this area, the United States owns a very serious advantage over Chinese markets. The US employs a free market system, while flawed, still represents an opportunity to catch new businesses on the rise to provide profits for investors. Chinese investors do not currently enjoy this opportunity. The Chinese stock market is highly regulated to protect investors from serious losses. The American stock market has no such safeguards.

The Chinese system automatically cuts off trading after a 10% rise or loss on any one given day. This has a few serious ramifications. It drastically reduces the potential to make any financial killings in one day or even in a few days. Conversely, it does protect the Chinese consumer from taking enormous losses in just one or a few days as well. The real bottom line is that the Chinese stock market is fairly boring and has a poor record of providing profits for its investors. This is a lethal combination.

The free market system of the United States is far more exciting, and, like gambling, has great rewards for the winners, and harsh consequences for those on the wrong side of investments. Both systems have massive amounts of manipulation and corruption, so those variables are fairly well-balanced. The Chinese economic system is tightly controlled by the CCP; this has both an upside and downside. The upside is that things get done quickly and without a lot of political backbiting, which is a standard of the American economic system. The CCP reacts quickly to both real economic emergencies, and to economic opportunities in other countries; the United States does not.

The downside to the Chinese system is that these same tight controls limit capital ventures of all types, restricts enormous profits (most of the time), and are far more inflexible than the American models. The inability of the CCP to prevent its brain drain in the high tech area is another serious economic drawback for its system. The CCP is currently trying to rectify all of these drawbacks, but it will take many years to make changes, and the coming century seems to place the United States in a superior position for the foreseeable future.

The US system favors the rich at the expense of the poor and working class. This is fine if you are rich or part of the middle class. It is not so great if you are part of the working class or poor. Millions of the working class, the ones who could least afford it, lost almost 90% of their investment capital in the last two economic meltdowns in the US, primarily caused by US investment bankers and misuse of derivatives. This, in turn, accelerated the losses incurred by the same working class (and millions of the middle class as well) in the real estate market in both crises.

The end result was millions of repossessed, bank-owned homes that now provide good buying opportunities for those with much more money than the previous owners; to wit, the middle class and the rich. A clear case of the rich get richer and the poor get poorer. The final result for the working class and poor was now homelessness, inferior apartment living instead of a small house, loss of at least 80% of savings and investments, and a general feeling that as one of these unfortunates, you were pretty much on your own, and that their government was not too much of a help.

Chinese banks are pretty much the same as US banks, but they generally do business like they are in the 1950s and 1960s. They have and use high-tech, but they also have a myriad of forms, paper files, and antiquated banking procedures left over from the mid-1900s. Some Chinese banks combine their postal services with their banking services in order to make a bit more money. All major Chinese banks are subsidized by the Chinese government and protected from the enormous losses taken from mandatory loans to small businesses. These small business loans fail at a rate of 92% according to the Bank of China.

Chinese banks are essentially safe and secure. Far fewer of them are robbed than are US banks, because guns are less readily available in China. Also, you would get a hernia trying to rob a Chinese bank, since the paper currency is only about as 1/6 as valuable as the US dollar. This means you would have to carry six times as much currency if you robbed a bank.

The primary note of currency for both countries is the 100 dollar bill. In the US it green and black and in China it is pink. The reason it is pink is that it saves money. The Chinese constantly strive to save money, while the US is a bit more wasteful in producing their currencies. The current value as of 2014 for the Chinese 100 Yuan bill is roughly about $15.00US. This means that the average Chinese has to carry around about six times as many bills as do Americans using the same amount of cash.

And cash is the primary mode of payment in China. There are credit cards and electronic payments made, but the Chinese prefer to primarily do business in cash. This leads to some very comical situations where some Chinese are carrying around massive stacks of 100RMB notes to make major purchases like cars and down payments on an apartment. Of course, it is much safer to carry around large amounts of cash in China than it is in the United States because of the lack of availability of guns.

Very few Chinese banks are internationalized, or partners with Western banks. China Construction Bank (CCB) used to be partnered with Bank of America until 2013. They still have a currency transfer agreement, but have eliminated all their other partnering ventures. Getting Chinese cash to the US and vice-versa is still a major problem in both China and the US. The future bodes well, however, for this problem to gradually be reconciled before this century is out. Banking reforms in both countries are trending toward a closer cooperation in internationalizing both currencies.

US banks are the bad boys of international banking because of their dismal behavior during the two last financial crises in the United States. Their atrocious record of unethical derivative banking practices has made both China and the rest of the world very wary of dealing with American investment banks and bankers. The more conservative elements of major American banking, however, are still in the forefront of international banking in several areas.

American banks offer several retirement plans that are not available in Chinese banks. This is a major advantage because older adults are the richest segment in every country in the world. A senior banking client is more likely to bank where they have their IRA or Retirement account.

Strategic Alliance Issues

When it comes to countries, strategic alliance issues generally revolve around two issues; national security and economic gain. Most often, national security takes precedence over alliances for economic gain. To that end, both the United States and China have followed different paths for both national security and economic gain in the 20th century, but will follow quite similar paths as we move through the 21st century.

In the 20th century, the United States was protected by two large oceans on either side of the country. These oceans still provide an obstacle to most military intrusions, but have been negated by the potential of both nuclear threat and terrorist activity. Consequently, the United States is now more concerned about terrorist activity than they are about any potential military threat against the country.

Economically, the United States used to be a manufacturing giant, but now they are receding in that area. China is currently the number one manufacturing giant in the world. The US has developed expertise in tech for the 21st century; an expertise they had developed as well during the 20th century in nuclear, electronic, and communication tech.

The United States produces more food per person than any other country in the world. The quality of American food and water is the highest in the world as well. This powerful combination of quantity and quality allows the US a great deal of leverage when allying with potential partners.

Traditional national security partners of the US in the 20th century were England, Canada, Mexico, Australia and various other countries. NATO, SEATO, and other international organizations were set up to preserve American national security as well. These scenarios have pretty much been replaced by Homeland Security and Interpol, as terrorism has now superseded military threat as the number one concern for national security.

In China during the 20th century, Russia was usually their number one ally. They were in constant conflict (and still are) with Japan for both land and trade. The 21st century sees a similar dependency. Russia needs China and vice-versa. Japan is still a threat. But terrorism is also beginning to rear its ugly head in China for the first time, early in this century. Muslims in Xinjiang are killing native Han Chinese and Han Chinese are killing Muslim as well. If China continues to see a proliferation of religious unrest in their substantial Muslim populations, it could signal a shift in national security concerns.

There isn't a country in the world that could defeat China in a land war. So military threat is not as much a concern for China as it has been in the 20th century. Terrorism and International Trade seem to be the current priorities for the Chinese government. Unfortunately, China has a weak Air Force and Navy and must face a Japan that has a superior Navy and at least an equal Air Force. Japan has been the traditional ally of the United States in Asia, but that scenario may be changing as well, if Japan keeps insisting on gearing up militarily.

The United States wants no part of Japanese military adventures and the US will not go to the mat with any foe (particularly China) of the Japanese if their military adventures get out of hand. The US does over 500 billion a year in trade with China and Japan does over 800 billion a year in trade with China. It would not pay for either country to upset that dynamic.

At this point in time, it would appear economic strategic alliances take precedence over military strategic alliances for both countries. China, however, has been quicker to realize this reality than the United States. To that end, the leaders of the CCP have created numerous highly profitable alliances with many countries in Africa and South America. The US has lagged badly in both these continents.

Based on current trends, unless the United States wakes up and initiates strong overtures to the dozens of countries that China has already allied with, China will gradually overtake the United States as the number one deal maker in the world. The United States will then be forced to become completely dependent on its tech expertise to the exclusion of all other markets in the world community. This might be a dangerous path for the United States to pursue in the future.

Future Scenarios

Continuation of the Status Quo

This scenario is both the most and least likely to occur. It is the most likely to occur because, as the old saying goes, the more things change, the more they stay the same. The rich will still stay rich, the poor will still be poor, there will still be senseless global conflicts in various parts of the world, and people will continue to struggle to move up in class. Conversely, time does not stand still, and the scenarios we now experience will all change with the inevitability of time passage. There will be new threats, opportunities, strengths and weaknesses to exploit or defend.

So if current trends continue, we can extrapolate some potential scenarios based on the possible end results of these trends.

If we continue to improve our food production as a world population, starvation and poor diet will continue to diminish by the end of the current century. The food will be more available, healthier, and more easily transported than it was in the previous century.

Unfortunately, our healthy water availability will lag behind our world food production. Global Warming, if left unchecked, will continue to dry up millions of acres of land that is now currently occupied. People from these lands will inevitably gravitate toward the cities, further exacerbating a crowed and unhealthy living environment for city-dwellers. Some progress is being made in this area, but we are projecting a status quo, (do nothing) scenario. That would mean a degrading of the world water supply.

Air quality will continue to degrade as well, unless quantum measures are taken against the consumption of fossil fuels. This will lead to more cases of cancer, lung disease and other health complications in the cities that will have pollutants in excess of acceptable levels (such as

Beijing, Shanghai, Hong Kong and others). Air quality will be slightly better in US cities because their populations are only about 25% of those in Chinese cities.

Housing in China will become cheaper at some point because the real estate bubble currently in effect will burst sooner or later, driving down real estate prices dramatically (in a similar fashion to the real estate drop in prices in the US after the 2008 bubble burst). People will lose billions of dollars in their investment portfolios in China, but this will be offset by the millions of Chinese families that will now be able to afford a new apartment.

Economically, the United States will continue to lose partnering opportunities to the Chinese because the Chinese are less restrictive in their negotiations. The Chinese do not tie in national defense concerns or require military bases in order to do business; the Americans will continue to lose market share here. However, in the area of tech, the US will continue to dominate the world to the end of the current century, if all current trends continue.

Eventually, both countries will assume a one and two position in world economic power. Which country will be number one and which will be number two is still unclear, but generally speaking, tech usually dominates other areas of economic development.

The US Superior Scenario

US citizens will like this premise, and Chinese citizens will most likely laugh at it, but this scenario is one in which the US miraculously recovers from its financial doldrums, magically begins to make inroads in deal-making with all of the other countries in the world that China has been to first and is currently gaining in market share, makes earth-shattering discoveries for the elimination of fossil fuels, increases food and clean water production, reduces pollution and global warming effects, creates new, dynamic technologies, and creates a sustainable non-tech economy that grows at steady rate to complement its tech economy. I also have a bridge in Brooklyn I would like to sell you if you think this is the most likely of all the future scenarios listed.

Militarily, the US is already, by far, the most dominant military power in the world. There is just one problem. The problems of the 21st century will seldom, be solved through military solutions. Terrorism cannot be solved with military intervention. Economic health cannot be achieved with the use of military force. At best, military options would be used for isolated outbreaks of unacceptable social behavior voted on by the UN, which would only require a minute segment of the US military. The rest could be replaced by local police forces (taking former military and turning them into local policemen would solve both problems at the same time). Guns would then be outlawed (as they are in China) reducing the crime rate by 90%+ and increasing productivity in the population by almost 5%.

The US will adopt bullet trains and become the number one producer of bullet trains in the world. People will be able to live hundreds of miles away in healthier environments and will only have to come to the cities to work. Cars will be completely free of fossil fuels and air pollution levels will go down by over 60%. Levels of lung disease, liver disease and cancers will be reduced by well over 20%.

The US, because of its economic superiority, will be able to export democracy to just about every other country in the world. English will increase as the international language of business. Terrorism will wane because the primary cause of terrorism is economic exclusion. If the US can spread its economic model of success throughout the world, it might signal a new era of world peace, never reached before by mankind. Everyone in the world will have clean air, clean water, plenty of food, and a job. And pigs will begin to fly (those would be capitalist pigs).

The China Superior Scenario

My Chinese friends and students will love this one, and my friends in the US should get a good chuckle from it. If everything breaks just the right way for China, they could be the leaders of the world by the end of the 21st century. This would require the following (among other variables) to take place: The exclusive invention of a super-weapon so destructive that it could annihilate an entire country in a matter of seconds, the continuation of current international deal-making to the extent that China becomes completely dominant as the world supplier of anything that requires a factory, the complete destruction of Japan with nuclear weapons, the development of Chinese basketball and baseball to the extent they become superior to American basketball and baseball, the elimination of the one-party system, the elimination of pollution, a job for everyone where they live (including the countryside), affordable housing, free public education for all up to the doctoral level, and a completely free-market economy.

Some additional benefits might be the elimination of Beijing Opera, no more chopsticks, the elimination of sexism in Chinese society, the elimination of two-hour naps at lunchtime (of course, if the Chinese are this successful, they might be able to take three hour naps instead of two), the elimination of motorcycles and scooters, the elimination of sidewalks used as highways, the elimination of alcohol poisoning, food poisoning and all other types of poison in the Chinese ecosystem, the elimination of cigarettes , the elimination of karaoke, the elimination of stinky tofu, the elimination of traffic, and the elimination of inconvenient inclement weather. In short, this is a highly unlikely scenario.

Realistically speaking, if China continues their successful country by country trade negotiations (they are the best in the world at this), they will at least have tons of money for the local economy. The flip side of this global strategy is that China will become less isolated and more vested in the world economy. This will leave them much more vulnerable to any future global crises, and not immune to global problems as they have been in the past. Terrorism is a perfect example. The Chinese never worried about it in the 20th century, but now it is a major concern for them in the 21st century because of Xinjiang and other areas.

IF China sustains its phenomenal economic growth, has a soft landing for its overpriced real estate bubble that will eventually burst, has the good fortune to discover a couple of new technologies (this is the least likely), and the US stumbles during the 21st century, THEN it may challenge the US for world economic superiority. It will still have to solve its problems with Japan, however, before any of this would be possible.

Third Party Superior Scenario

A very unlikely scenario, but one that is mathematically possible, is a third party, not the US or China as the world economic leader by the end of the 21st century. From the group of suspects that are left over from the top six economies in the world, we would have to consider the following: Russia, England, Germany and Japan. Of these, the one most likely to be the third party superior would be Germany. Why? Because it is head and shoulders over the other three in technology.

It is a well-known fact that Germany has the best engineers in the world. They developed the atom bomb, space travel and the best cars ever devised by man in the 20th century. There is no reason to believe that they cannot take all that money that they save on national defense and reinvest it in developing new technologies to drive their economy to the top of the charts. Japan used this same strategy with some variations during the seventies and eighties and achieved a high degree of economic success.

Japan could do it again, but because it currently seems hell-bent on militarization, that could seriously derail any movement toward the top of the economic food chain in the foreseeable future. Even in the best of economic times, without any military budget, Japan has often been deficient in tech. Their strength lies in making the lowest-priced item that has a moderate amount of quality; the same successful formula used by Walmart.

England is probably the least likely of the entire group. Lacking in substantial natural resources, and locked into costly national defense agreements with the US, England just does not have the resources to compete with the top three or four economies in the world.

Russia has enormous natural resources in gas and all mining items. It has stabilized considerably over the last twenty years and is even gaining back some of the territory it lost during the breakup of the Soviet Union (see Ukraine) . However, the one-party system and massive corruption still plague the Russian economy. It may challenge again in the 22nd century, but it is a fairly safe bet to say they will not challenge for the top spot in the 21st century.

Germany continues to be the frontrunner because of its tech capabilities. Some find it puzzling that they have lagged in tech communications, hardware and software, but that could turn around at any given moment with just a few major advances or discoveries. Any country that can develop the atom bomb, space travel and the best cars in the world, can also develop just about anything it puts its mind to.

Partnership Scenario

An intriguing scenario might be the partnering of two of the superpowers for the purpose of world economic dominance in the 21st century. A truly sensible and useful scenario, but one that is not very likely because of the national pride that is always present in each major power's psyche. Most countries would rather fail by themselves than succeed with the help of others. This idiotic stance is, unfortunately, the modus operandi of most major economies. Modern companies realize the importance of partnering to stay on top; modern countries are not quite as smart because of politics.

But if the economic reward was great enough, even the politicians of the major powers could be swayed to give superpower partnerships a whirl. The most devastating world partnership would easily be a United States-China linking that would be virtually impossible for even the next six to ten economies of the world to compete with, even if they partnered with each other (which is very unlikely as well).

The effect of a US-China partnership would be profound. There would little or no chance of a military challenge from any one or even group of countries in the world. This partnership would almost completely dominate the economic landscape. The quality of US goods with the low labor costs of China would be an unbeatable combination if put into effect. Both countries would completely dominate North and South America, Africa and Asia. Most of the Mideast would be under their domain as well. Only Europe would be able to hold off this economic beast, but not for very long. Eventually, Europe would come to economic subservience as well.

Russia would become dangerously isolated and might respond in a not-to-friendly manner to either or both partners. But in the end, Russia could not challenge such a strong partnership and would eventually come to tow as well.

The ultra partnership would be unlikely to occur, however, because of the major political differences between the two countries. Democracy and Socialism have a lot of common ground, but pure capitalism and pure communism are pretty far apart on the economic scale. Most likely, their will be cooperation somewhere in the middle, falling short of a complete partnership.

48

Economic Superior Scenario

The interesting thing about the economic superior scenario is that either the US or China could wind up in that position, given the right set of circumstances and variables. Let us examine how both countries would possibly act under such circumstances.

The US now enjoys current economic superiority in a number of areas in the world. The US dollar is most often employed as the monetary unit for the vast majority of countries that do large volumes of trade. The term "in US dollars" is almost always employed by every major government. But past performance in economics does not guarantee future results. Look at Egypt, Greece, Rome, Spain, and England; the five predecessors of economic leadership in world history. All of them rose, and all of them fell to another foreign power.

As sad as they may seem to be for Americans, it is a source of hope and anticipation for the Chinese. China is poised to be the next economic superstar of world history by the end of the 21st century, but there are many variables that can go wrong and derail that dream. Assuming the US is able to maintain a certain amount of tech growth for the balance of the century, it should still be in the driver's seat by the end of it.

If the US is the economic superior of the world by the end of the century, the world will be a bit different than it is now. The dollar will rule supreme in every corner of the earth. English will continue to be the language of business and the most dominant language on the planet. But these two variables already exist. What would change by the end of the century is the impression that the US model is the right economic model (and possibly the only economic model), and that the rest of the countries of the world will either have to learn the American way of doing business, or they will suffer economically.

Right now, that impression is a bit clouded by the economic success of the Chinese. Dozens of countries are choosing the Chinese model for doing business and trade because it is purely business and not related to national defense or preconditions, as is negotiating with the US. Several countries in South America and Africa have already benefited by making massive deals with the Chinese, with several of them making billions of dollars for both parties. That is one of the not so secret ingredients of the Chinese model; it practically ensures that the other party will benefit greatly economically from any partnership. The US model depends too much on military protection rather than sound business principles.

If China is the economic superior of the world by the end of the century, the world will be a much different place than it is now. People will take the RMB much more seriously, and it will not only become the fourth most important currency in the world, it might become the second or third most important currency. Or maybe even the most important currency. The odds are against it, but mathematically, it could happen.

If it did happen, then there would be a lot of changes in the way banks and people do business. The American model would suffer the most; the Euro would be devastated. The Pound would suffer as well. The Japanese Yen would have immense difficulties, as nothing would please the Chinese more than to drive Japan into bankruptcy. Japan, however, might not go peacefully into the night under this scenario. But China would take that chance.

The Chinese language might have a bit of a renaissance, but most Western countries will still ignore it like they do now, except for banks and businesses. The Chinese economic model will be politically attacked in the West as "artificial, government-controlled, one-dimensional, unimaginative, dangerous", and various other negative adjectives that have very little effect on the bottom line. The bottom line would still be, who makes the most money. The country that makes the most money wins. The end. Politics, religion and every other variable will be pushed to the backburner

The Military Superior Scenario

Realistically speaking, only the US has the possibility of becoming the leader of the world through military superiority. Up to this point in time, every military leader in world history has fallen (just like every economic world leader in history) to another country that eventually develops a superior technology or other strategy that obtains the top perch for them in the pecking order. Sadly, it must happen, sooner or later, to the US as well.

But this is not likely mathematically to happen by the end of this century. Given the current strength of the American military, its technical expertise, and its likelihood of continued development of technical expertise, the US should still be the military leader of the world until at least the end of the 21st century.

This is both good news and bad news. The good news is that the US will be the world leaders because of their military might. A lot of countries will resent this (many already do) and will purposely avoid dealing with the US on moral grounds. The bad news is that the US economic model will be sneered at, and the military model will be copied assiduously. If this is fine with the American public and the American business community, then the US will be in pretty much in the same position as the Roman Empire near the end of its long reign; highly feared, but not greatly respected.

However, if the US can develop an economic model that compliments its military superiority (unlike the Romans), it can continue to dominate for continued centuries. Regardless of what the US does or does not do, several other countries will continue to oppose its military and economic strategies. Unless there is a quantum jump in military technology by a foreign power, the US should stay firmly in control of its military superiority. With the US in the driver's seat for tech as well, the future bodes well for maintenance of the status quo.

China may, at some point in time, become militarily dominant in the Asian theater, but it has too many negative variables working against it to become the dominant military leader of the world. It has lost many more wars than it has won, it has a mass xenophobic mentality when it comes to military adventures (for good reasons), it has never really defeated Japan in a war by itself (without US nuclear assistance, China would have suffered the loss of over half its territory to Japan, as well as many additional millions of deaths before a conventional end to World War 2), the Japanese Navy is far more experienced and skilled than the Chinese Navy, and has a historical record of dominance over the Chinese, Australia is an absolutely untouchable ally of England and the US and guarantees the presence of both countries in Asia (China has no such entrée into Europe or the Americas), and China would be (at this point in time) uncomfortable in a military leadership role outside of Asia.

China has had far more success with business than it has had militarily in Asia and other parts of the world. Soldiers traditionally hold a very low place on the pecking order in Chinese society. Businessmen used to be held in even lower esteem in Chinese history than soldiers, but that condition of society has changed radically, as business and getting rich are now far more important in China than any other variable of Chinese life. Confucianism has been replaced by naked capitalism. People who want to get rich and make money do not become involved in wars and politics. They can take advantage of people and countries that do have too many wars, and too much international political intrigue. I think you can guess one or two of the countries I am talking about. (baseball and vodka are popular in them).

US Superior Strategic Alliance Scenario

In the order of likelihood, England, Canada, Mexico, South America, Germany, Europe, and then China represent the highest percentages of countries and regions to partner with the US until the end of the 21st century. This data is based on historical, economic and political histories, events and traditions. There is nothing to prevent any one of these countries or regions to go to the front of the line, but the current order is the most likely mathematically.

England has been a historical, economic and political partner (not to mention military partner) of the US for the last hundred years or so. Geologically and historically speaking, that is really not a long time. However, it is still the most likely partnership in the next fifty or so years for the United States.

Generally speaking, the US has gone down the economic road by itself in the last hundred years or so and will most likely continue to do so in the immediate and not-too-immediate future as well. England only seems to be called upon during military crises and is practically ignored when the US is considering economic options. At this point in time in Europe, Germany is a far more attractive partner economically than is England.

Canada is close by, but is far too tepid in tech development for the US to seriously consider them as a major economic partner. The same holds true for Mexico and South America. The European Union is an option for the US, but why have to deal with all the weak economies within the European Union, when it is clear that Germany is, by far, the strongest economy in the group?

That leaves China as a logical alternative.

But, there is one serious flaw in the Chinese economy that China must overcome in order to be seriously considered by the US as its primary partner; technological development. Germany is renowned for tech and China is famous for copying it. Unless China can provide its substantial brain trust in its own country with the intellectual property protection it needs, its technocrats will continue to flee by the millions to other advanced countries. This extremely costly brain drain will then preclude China from achieving the status of a technologically advanced country that would be considered a suitable partner for the US.

My money is on Germany or the US going it alone.

China Superior Strategic Alliance

China has its own requirements for a potential partner for world domination economically or both economically and militarily. Since it is highly unlikely that no partner on earth can offer China military superiority over the US, it will most likely go the economic route to try and get the best of the US with a powerhouse partner. That partner, at this point in time, is none other than the same partner that would most likely benefit the US the most; Germany.

China will never seriously partner with Japan or any other country in Asia. Only India is an outside possibility in Asia. Those two would be a formidable duo both in Asia and on the world economic horizon. The combined populations of India and China would dwarf any other alliance and the combination of English and tech that India could provide would nicely augment the low production costs and order that Chinese society provides.

Outside of Asia, the US is too politically removed from Chinese sensibilities to be a serious contender as the primary partner. The US taste for military adventures goes against the grain of Chinese cooperation initiatives. India scores much better in this category as well. The Chinese distrust the Russians even more than the Americans. The US never threatened China with nuclear weapons, but Russia did in the 1960s. So Russia will never be an option for China.

That brings us to Germany. Outside of India, Germany is the only country capable of massive tech development and it is more stable politically than India. The rift between Hindus and Muslims is a problem China would like to avoid, as they have a large Muslim population of their own. Germany has no such rift, politically or religiously. Germany's tech is also superior to that of India's tech as well.

An alliance of Germany and China, just as an alliance of Germany and the US, would be an extremely formidable foe. One of the major stumbling blocks in this scenario, however, is Germany's membership in the European Union. China would demur from joining the European Union as a major partner for the same reasons that the US would not consider it; why include all those weak economies along with the strong German economy? Ultimately, it is Germany that must decide whether to leave the European Union and partner with the US or China. It will be the most important decision Germany will make in the 21st century. So, Germany or India?

This one is too close to call.

Unknown Tech Advance Scenario

At this point in time, there are only two countries on the face of the planet that have high percentage chances of success for creating a future jump in tech superiority. Those two countries would be the United States and Germany. If both countries were to seriously partner, the rest of the world would have practically no chance to compete with the combination of those two tech superpowers.

But let's take the approach of the most likely percentage scenario; the one where each superpower keeps to itself primarily for the balance of the century and only makes limited partnerships with other countries on a one company at a time basis. That would mean that either the US or Germany would then assume the mantle of the world's leader in tech.

The US currently holds the upper hand, primarily because of companies like Microsoft, Apple, Intel and a few others, but one can hardly dismiss the country that is renowned for its engineers and its great historical contributions to tech. Einstein came from Germany, as did Oppenheimer, the father of the atom bomb. Werner Von Braun came from Germany and helped create the American space program. Dismiss Germany in tech at your own peril.

If the US becomes the country to make the next giant leap in tech, the economic repercussions will be profound. There will be an explosion of companies that will be responsible for the production, distribution and sales of the new product. There will be millions of jobs added to the American economy. It will be like the old 1990s all over again, when most people in the US were making money and had a fine home to live in.

The US will greatly influence other world economies as well with this new technology. Countries friendly to the US in both political and military affairs will get first priority. China will do better than Russia in this scenario, because the US feels more secure with China than it does with Russia. Europe will benefit as well as a traditional ally of the US. Areas of the world that will be last in line for the new tech will include Russia, Japan, the Mideast, Africa, and South America. Mexico and Canada will benefit by pure luck because they border the US.

If Germany creates the next great breakthrough in tech, things will be a bit different. Germany will take more of a mercenary view and not be as obsessed with military alliances as is the US. The European Union will benefit greatly from a German breakthrough, and once again, Russia will be left to fend for itself. China and India will benefit more than Japan because they are not a threat to the German car industry. The rest of Asia will have to fend for themselves, but generally have good economic ties with Germany. Africa and South America will fare better with Germany as the new tech leader as well. The Mideast will, once again, be at the mercy of the West.

The Chaos Scenario

This is the least attractive and least likely of all the future scenarios of China-US in 2100. That would be one where no country is a clear leader of tech, military or political power in the world and where no two great powers have partnered to bring world order to the forefront.

This would be a messy world, where terrorists could run rampant, where there was economic instability in the majority of the developed nations and the certainty of instability in the undeveloped nations. It would not be a pleasant time or place to live in.

There are a few major variables that could contribute to a chaos scenario. The foremost would be the inability of countries to cooperate politically, economically and militarily. But there are other negative variables to consider as well. A new disease that has no vaccine could develop in any given decade. The Black Plague killed over one third of Europe. The Flu epidemic of the late 1910s killed almost 15% of the world population. A pandemic could influence world economic leadership, but the percentages are against that particular scenario.

There could be a major war. This would wipe out a few decades of tech and economic advancement in just a matter of minutes if the scale of the war was nuclear. This too, is a highly unlikely scenario.

Actually, given all the current data and the movement away from militarism and toward economic cooperation, the chaos theory remains one of the less likely to occur. But if it did, then being a survivalist would come in very handy. Those fortunate enough to have land and the weapons to defend it would have the best chance of survival. The cities would be an unimaginable place of horror to live in as there would be a mass exodus to the countryside. Well over 90% of the city dwellers would perish if all government and social services broke down.

Robberies would be commonplace and gangs would be formed for survival. Gangs would eventually rule the streets of the cities as law enforcement would break down. There would some type of survival, but only a few steps above wild animals. There would not be a lot of roving gangs in the countryside because fuel would become very scarce and transportation would be a problem. This is another reason that countryside dwellers who were well-armed and living in small enclaves would have a better chance than those living in the cities. Suicide rates would increase dramatically. Not a place you or I would like to be.

Some Final Notes

To sum up, the most likely scenarios are the ones that are currently trending. The variables will always be the same, with one or two new ones added every decade. Generally speaking, however, the primary variables of economics, politics, and military action will most likely dominate the variables.

The most likely countries to emerge or reemerge in the latter half of the 21st century detected from these algorithms are the United States, China, Germany, Russia, Japan, and England. Since there are only a handful (6) of countries that could emerge from these variables, the number of possibilities for future scenarios is really not that varied.

Regardless of who emerges as the world economic leader, they will be facing several serious short-term and long term problems. Global warming is not going away. The dependency on fossil fuels is not going away. Pollution will still be a major issue. Corruption will continue to be a serious drain on several economies.

But most of all, the issue of exclusion must be examined and treated, like any other disease. Religious exclusion, racial exclusion, nationalistic exclusion, economic exclusion, and all other types of exclusion tend to polarize and diminish potentially healthy economies. From small villages to small cities, exclusion will continue to remain a problem. Those who are able to solve the exclusion problem first, will become the next leaders of the world order. I wonder who it will be?

www.ingramcontent.com/pod-product-compliance
Lightning Source LLC
Chambersburg PA
CBHW060341290526
45793CB00003B/681